AN ANSWER TO
ANGER AND FRUSTRATION

by

Norman Wright

Harvest House Publishers
Irvine, California 92714

Scripture quotations taken from the New American Standard Bible © 1960, 1962, 1968, 1971, The Lockman Foundation. Used by permission.

Scripture quotations taken from The Amplified Bible: Old Testament © Zondervan Corp.; The Amplified Bible: New Testament © 1958, The Lockman Foundation. Used by permission.

Scripture quotations taken from The Living Bible © 1971, Tyndale House Publishers. Used by permission.

AN ANSWER TO
ANGER AND FRUSTRATION

© 1977 by Harvest House Publishers,
Irvine, CA 92714
Library of Congress Catalog Card
Number 76-51531
ISBN 0-89081-030-3

Printed in the United States of America

FRUSTRATION

Frustrated! No matter what you want to do, no matter what you try, nothing seems to work.

Frustration is an inevitable human feeling. It is a condition of wanting something and not getting it. Frustration can occur when our goals or desires are blocked. It can also be just the opposite—when we don't want something and have it forced upon us.

Frustration can also be related to expectations. When we do a kind act for someone, we expect it to be recognized and even reciprocated. When this expectation is not fulfilled, frustration and then anger can occur. In fact, frustration and anger are closely related much of the time.

Have you ever . . .

. . . worn yourself out cleaning the house all day and no one noticed?

. . . spent two hours fixing yourself up hoping he would notice and perhaps suggest going out to dinner, but nothing happened?

. . . brought your wife a surprise gift (an expensive one, at that) and then saw no excitement on her face?

. . . worked for days on a project and the boss took it for granted and never even said thanks?

. . . taken the kids on a special outing and all they did was bicker and fight?

. . . left an hour early to avoid the rush hour traffic just to discover thousands of other motorists did the same thing?

. . . wanted to share your excitement over a new experience you had that day but your spouse and children weren't interested?

. . . had a day off and wanted to sleep in but you woke up bright and early and couldn't get back to sleep?

You probably have your own list of frustrations. Take a few minutes right now and write down twelve situations which frustrate you the most. After you have done that, write down how you usually respond to these frustrations.

HANDLING FRUSTRATION

Now that you have considered your own frustrations, let's consider a popular myth about frustration: *Frustration always upsets a person!* That is not true. Frustration *does not* always make a person upset, disturbed, or angry! It depends upon the individual. If we think and plan carefully before a frustrating situation occurs, our predetermined course of action can help us avoid an anger reaction. So much of our disturbance and anger can be attributed to our thought life and our expectations. *It is possible to accept frustrations without becoming upset.*

Dr. Paul Hauck, a psychotherapist, put it this way: "Millions of frustrations are far more easily tolerated than we usually think. Children not finishing their dinner is not an awful frustration, just the waste of a few cents. And if a few cents bothers you, put the plate in the refrigerator until later. A person swerving in front of you in traffic is not doing something that calls for a nuclear explosion. It isn't awful to have someone honking his horn impolitely behind you—it's only slightly annoying. Not getting your raise can hurt your pocketbook but not you, unless you let it. And that's the point, isn't it? Frustrations are not usually earthshaking to begin with—they can be tolerated quite nicely if we make the effort. Secondly, frustrations, even if they *are* severe, don't have to lead to disturbances unless we allow them to." [1]

One way to handle frustration is to accept it as being as inevitable as death. Frustra-

1. Paul Hauck, *Overcoming Frustration and Anger* (Philadelphia: Westminster Press, 1974), p. 65.

tions are a part of life. Why be so surprised when they occur? You can choose to look at a frustration as a catastrophy or as an opportunity for growth. It is your own choice.

THE BIBLE AND FRUSTRATION

The scripture provides some insight into the problem of frustration. Several passages indicate the proper response that we should have to frustration:

"Consider it wholly joyful, my brethren, whenever you are enveloped in or encounter trials of any sort, or fall into various temptations. Be assured and understand that the trial and proving of your faith bring out endurance and steadfastness and patience" (James 1:2-3, Amplified).

"(You should) be exceedingly glad on this account, though now for a little while you may be distressed by trials and suffer temptations, so that (the genuineness) of your faith may be tested" (I Peter 1:6-7, Amplified).

"Blessed, happy, to be envied is the man who is patient under trial and stands up under temptation, for when he has stood the test and been approved he will receive (the victor's) crown of life which God has promised to those who love Him" (James 1:12, Amplified).

Many temptations are frustrations and some frustrations can become temptation to sin. But the Word of God indicates the attitude that we should have in these situations.

THE SOURCE OF FRUSTRATION

Frustration occurs in many forms. You may experience frustration in the area of your wishes, desires, ambitions, hopes, hungers, instinct, or even your will. You may often respond with anger. If you are hungry and cannot eat, you may become angry. If you are frightened by something and cannot run away, you may become angry. If you want to join a certain club and cannot, you may become angry.

When you are frustrated, you must consider the source of your frustration. Objects, situations, or other people may be the cause. Your friends, father, mother, wife, husband, children, or employer could be the source of frustration. You can be frustrated just as easily by someone you dislike as by the one you love most.

You could also be frustrated by what some call the laws of nature. If you are hungry, you could be frustrated by an empty refrigerator. If you have looked forward to playing tennis on your first day off in three weeks and it rains on that day, you will be disappointed and frustrated.

Even your values or moral system can frustrate you and deter you from fulfilling certain desires. Some Christians have been heard to say, "If only I weren't a Christian, I could do that and really enjoy it!" Even though this person wants to retain his value system, it can be very frustrating. Sometimes we tend to blame God for our frustration because we feel that He places too many limitations upon us or does not give us what we think we deserve.

FRUSTRATION AND ANGER

Why does frustration lead to anger? The basic assumptions that we have about life can cause anger to arise out of frustration. Frustration may begin with the desire for something—"I want something." Now, desires are natural; we all have wants and desires. We set goals and we want them to come true. But we must distinguish between "I want something" and "I must have it." If you can distinguish between the two, you may not become so upset.

When we say "I want something" we are sometimes saying, "I must have it. I've got to have it or else. If I don't get it, it's going to be awful. I've got to have my way, and if anyone blocks me they are terrible. In fact, if they don't let me get my way, then that's just a sign that they don't love me." These statements only help create anger within us. We assume that we have to have our way and are frustrated because this should not happen to us.

Perhaps we should ask the question, "Why not?" Why shouldn't we experience frustration just like anyone else? We are not immune to it. It can be a growth experience. And it will be if we add another phrase to the initial statement, "I want something." "I want something, but it is all right if I don't get it. It is not the end of the world. I can live without it and can adjust and find an alternative."

Learning to live without something can often bring a greater level of satisfaction to our lives. This is not to say that we totally give up and never forge ahead. It is just that we do not allow ourselves to become upset by the various frustrations of life. If we do, the result is an emotional response which most people call anger.

Here are some statements that people have made indicating their wants or desires.

Space has been provided for you to write a response to each statement. Your response should help you accept the possibility of the particular desire not being fulfilled.

For example, "I want my husband to notice the clean house that I've spent seven hours slaving over today." If the husband does not notice the clean house, the wife may either give him the cold shoulder or a vesuvian eruption over his lack of sensitivity, consideration, and appreciation.

The following statement might help the wife to accept her husband's lack of appreciation: "I want my husband to notice the clean house that I've spent seven hours slaving over today. But if he doesn't, that is all right too. My happiness and sense of satisfaction do not depend upon his response. I did not clean it up solely for his response but because it needed to be cleaned. I feel better about the house and my effort. His appreciation would just be an added benefit."

Under each statement below, write a response that you could make to yourself in your own mind that would help you accept the frustration.

1. "I want to be sure to get to the sale at the store before everything is picked over. It is the only opportunity to save that much money."

2. "I sure hope that dinner is ready when I get home tonight and the kids keep quiet for a change. I don't need any hassle today."

3. "After all of the work that I've put in on that committee, I hope that I'm considered for the chairmanship this year. It means a lot to me to be able to lead that group, if given the chance."

4. "I've just got to get this work done today before our guests arrive. I don't know what I'll do if they arrive before I finish."

5. "After giving my son piano lessons for seven years and paying all that money, I certainly hope that he doesn't ask to quit. Last year at this time he really hassled me about it. I just don't need that."

Now consider another step that can lessen the amount of frustration that you experience. When you want something, do you let others know about it or is it an unspoken expectation? Other people are not mind readers and they will not know what you want unless you share it with them. Telling the children or your spouse what you expect assists them in meeting your needs. Often they are grateful because you brought your desires out into the open. And if they do not respond as you expected, you do not have to become angry. You can learn to adjust and adapt. You can also learn to communicate your needs to them in a clearer and more positive manner. This will increase the likelihood of your desires being fulfilled. If one approach does not work, try another.

ANGER

Since frustration may cause anger, we ought to consider exactly what we mean by anger. The American Heritage Dictionary describes anger as a strong, usually temporary displeasure but does not specify the manner of expressions. You can be just as angry while keeping silent as you can while yelling at someone.

The words *rage* and *fury* are used to describe intense, uncontained, explosive emotion. Fury is thought of as being destructive but rage can be considered justified by certain circumstances.

Another word for anger is *wrath*—fervid anger that seeks vengeance or punishment. *Resentment* is usually used to signify suppressed anger brought about by a sense of grievance. *Indignation* is a feeling which results when you see the mistreatment of someone or something which is very important to you.

A simple definition of anger is a strong feeling of irritation or displeasure.

The Word of God has much to say about anger and uses a number of words to describe the various types of anger. In the Old Testament, the word for anger actually meant "nostril" or "nose." In ancient Hebrew psychology, the nose was thought to be the seat of anger. The phrase "slow to anger" literally means "long of nose." Synonyms used in the Old Testament for anger include ill-humor and rage (Esther 1:12), overflowing rage and fury (Amos 1:11), and indignation (Jer. 15:17). The emotion of anger can be the subject of the scripture even though the exact word is not present. Anger can be implied through words such as revenge, cursing, jealousy, snorting, trembling, shouting, raving, and grinding the teeth.

Several words are used for anger in the New Testament. It is important to note the distinction between these words. Many people have concluded that the scripture contradicts itself because in one verse we are taught not to be angry and in another we are admonished to "be angry and sin not." Which is correct and which should we follow?

One of the words used most often for anger in the New Testament is *Thumas*. It describes anger as a turbulent commotion or a boiling agitation of feelings. This type of anger blazes up into a sudden explosion. It is an outburst from inner indignation and is similar to a match which quickly ignites into a blaze but then burns out rapidly. This type of anger is mentioned twenty times in passages such as Ephesians 4:31 and Galatians 5:20. We are to control this type of anger.

Another type of anger mentioned only three times in the New Testament, and never in a positive sense, is *Parorgismos*. This is anger that has been provoked. It is characterized by irritation, exasperation, or embitterment.

". . . do not ever let your wrath—your exasperation, your fury or indignation—last until the sun goes down" (Eph. 4:26b, Amplified).

"Again I ask, Did Israel not understand?— Did the Jews have no warning that the Gospel was to go forth to the Gentiles, to all the earth? First, there is Moses who says, I will make you jealous of those who are not a nation; with a foolish nation I will make you angry" (Rom. 10:19, Amplified).

The most common New Testament word for anger is *Orge*. It is used forty-five times and means a more settled and long lasting attitude which is slower in its onset but more enduring. It often includes revenge. This kind of anger is similar to coals on a barbecue slowly warming up to red and then white hot and holding this temperature until the cooking is done.

There are two exceptions where this word is used and revenge is not included in its meaning. In Ephesians 4:26b we are taught not to "let the sun go down on your anger" (NASB). Mark 3:5 records Jesus as having looked upon the Pharisees "with anger" (NASB). In these two verses the word means an abiding and sealed habit of the mind which is aroused under certain conditions against evil and injustice. This is the type of anger that Christians are encouraged to have—the anger that includes no revenge.

The basic overall theme of scripture concerning anger is that it will be a part of life. It is not to be denied, but it is to be controlled. Certain types of anger are not healthy and should be put away. Anger should be aroused against definite injustices and then used properly.

What about the type of anger that you experience? What is it like? How would you classify it as you read over these definitions again? Take a few moments right now and try to think of some examples of each of these types of anger in your own life. Write down the situation and circumstances and describe the results of this anger.

Describe how you felt at the time and the reaction of others to you.

THE RESULTS OF ANGER

What are the results of anger? Are they constructive or destructive? If they are destructive, do they have to be? How does anger affect one's body? How does it affect family life?

Anger motivates a person to hate, wound, damage, annihilate, despise, scorn, disdain, loathe, vilify, curse, despoil, ruin, demolish, abhor, abominate, desolate, ridicule, tease, kid, get even with, laugh at, humiliate, goad, shame, criticize, scold, bawl out, irritate, beat up, fight, compete with, crush, offend, or bully another person. All of these are definitely negative!

The first time we see the effects of anger in the scripture, they are very destructive. "But for Cain and his offering He had no respect or regard. So Cain was exceedingly angry and indignant, and he looked sad and depressed. And the Lord said to Cain, Why are you angry?" (Gen. 4:5-6a, Amplified).

Cain was angry at his brother. Why? Because Abel's sacrifice was acceptable and his was not. Inwardly Cain experienced anger; the result was murder (4:8). Cain was alienated from his brother, from others, and from God. His anger led to murder and to extreme loneliness.

In another instance in the scripture we find an example of a father who, because of his displaced anger, almost killed his son. Saul was angry, envious and jealous of David. The scripture describes the scene: "Then Saul's anger was kindled against Jonathan, and he said to him, You son of a perverse, rebellious woman, do not I know that you have chosen the son of Jesse to your own shame, and to the shame of your mother who bore you? But Saul cast his spear at him to smite him, by which Jonathan knew that his father had determined to kill David" (I Sam. 20:30, 33, Amplified).

One of the results of anger is violence toward family members. It occurred in the scripture and it occurs everyday. Today, police receive more calls for family conflicts than they do for aggravated assault, murder and all other serious crimes put together. Over 60 percent of the homicides committed in our nation are against family members. Even the police departments are concerned about responding to calls for family conflicts because 26 percent of police fatalities occur while handling family disturbance calls!

One Christian writer described the results of anger in her own life: "I remember blaming everyone else. It was never my fault. I only started screaming after someone else had provoked me. I staunchly maintained my innocence and was very defensive about the whole matter. I lived out each day in anger. I was mad at God, mad at myself, mad at others, and fit to be tied with the angry frustrations of life in general.

"Anger, during those disastrous beginning years of our marriage, wrote its name across my face in hard, dark, indelible lines. It announced to the world that it was my master controller. For me, looking into a mirror was an awful thing each day because I could see the creeping, ugly lines of anger aging my face. I not only feared growing old, but I was furious because I could see it happening. I was in my early 20's but my face was aging at an alarming rate!

"What anger did to my looks, however, was nothing compared to the atrocities it perpetrated on my emotions and my mind. Every outburst of temper took its unbelievable toll on my character and personality.

"As a woman, I became closed-minded and opinionated about everyone from the butcher to the girls in the P.T.A. I made instant judgments and assumptions on everything from convenience foods to politics." [2]

2. Joyce Landorf, *The Fragrance of Beauty* (Wheaton, Ill.: Victor Books, 1973), pp. 108-9.

Paul Hauck said that reacting with anger is like throwing a cactus at someone with your bare hands; he may get hurt, but so will you!

HANDLING ANGER

One of the best reasons for not getting angry is that anger actually prevents a person from solving problems. It is not a solution to frustration but a reaction to frustration. If your spouse is after you to work on your marriage relationship or spend more time with the children, the solution is to talk about it. Find out how your spouse really feels, and do as much as you can to enhance your marriage relationship.

If you don't like your working conditions, you either attempt to improve the working atmosphere, learn to live with an undesirable, but not intolerable situation, or look for another job. Getting angry in either setting will not bring about positive, lasting improvements in which all parties are satisfied.

One way of dealing with anger is to approach it from the perspective of frustration. If anger has been brought about by frustration, it will have a tendency to disappear if the frustration is removed. If a child is having a fit because he can't have a candy bar, he will tend to control himself if the parent succumbs to his antics and gives him the candy. If a man is angry because a planned fishing trip may be suddenly cancelled, he will tend to quiet down if he is able to take that trip. If you are angry because a child is not responding to your attempts at discipline, your anger will subside when he begins behaving. The point to remember is that the energy of anger does not have to be unleashed in a manner that will hurt or destroy. Instead it can be used in a constructive manner to eliminate the frustration. If the original frustration cannot be eliminated, many individuals learn to accept substitute goals and thereby find nearly as much and sometimes even greater satisfaction.

Becoming hateful and desiring revenge is only a short step beyond being angry. Anger is usually accompanied by thoughts of how to get even with the other person instead of how to love that person and help him respond in a way that would be positive. How can we make a friend out of someone who is angry at us? Reacting with anger is like pouring gasoline on a fire that is already blazing. A chemical retardant would be far better! Proverbs 15:1 illustrates an appropriate response. "A soft answer turns away wrath; but grievous words stir up anger" (NASB).

This verse does not say that the other's anger will be turned away immediately, but in time it will happen. Remember that you will have to plan your verbal and nonverbal response to this person well in advance and even practice it if you expect it to happen. If you wait until you are in the heat of the altercation, you will not (and cannot because of physical changes) be able to change your old angry way of reacting. Visualizing and practicing the scriptural teaching in advance prepares you to make the proper response.

Why do you become angry at your family members when they don't respond to you? Why do you get angry at the kids when they don't pick up their room, mow the lawn, or dry the dishes properly?

Anger expressed by yelling at a son who does not mow the lawn carefully does not teach him how to do it correctly. Angry words directed to a sloppy daughter do not teach her how to be neat! Step by step instruction (even if it has been given before) can help solve the problem.

Another result of anger is that you become a carrier of a very infectious germ—anger itself! If you respond in anger, others around you can easily catch the germ. If you become angry at your spouse, don't be surprised if he or she responds in like manner! You gave your husband or wife an example to follow.

Your spouse is responsible for his or her own emotional responses but you still modeled the response. Perhaps if you respond with a kind but firm response, your spouse could follow this example.

Proverbs 22:24-25 illustrates this principle: "Make no friendships with a man given to anger, and with a wrathful man do not associate, lest you learn his ways and get yourself into a snare" (Amplified). "A man of wrath stirs up strife, and a man given to anger commits and causes much transgression" (Prov. 29:22, Amplified).

ANGER AND YOUR BODY

Have you ever considered what happens to your body when you experience anger? Many physical changes occur. Sugar pours into the system, creating energy. Your blood pressure increases, your heart beats faster, and blood containing needed nourishment circulates more rapidly through your body. Your blood clots much more quickly than normal. Additional adrenalin is released. The pupils of your eyes dilate which mobilizes you for action. Your muscles tense up—in fact, the muscles at the outlet of the stomach can squeeze down so tightly that it is difficult for anything to leave your stomach while you are angry. The digestive tract can become so spastic that severe pains are felt during or after the time you are angry.

Your blood pressure may increase from 130 to 230. Your heart beats faster—often up to 220 or higher. People have had strokes during a fit of anger because of the increased blood pressure. During anger, the arteries of the heart can squeeze down hard enough to produce angina pectoris or even a fatal coronary attack.

Dr. Leo Madow stated, "Hemorrhage of the brain is usually caused by a combination of hypertension and cerebral arteriosclerosis. It is sometimes called apoplexy or stroke and may have a strong emotional component, as is shown by such expressions as 'Apoplectic with rage' and 'Don't get so mad, you'll burst a blood vessel!' Anger can produce the hypertension which explodes the diseased cerebral artery, and a stroke results. Not only does repressed anger produce physical symptoms from headaches to hemorrhoids, but it can also seriously aggravate already existing physical illnesses. Even if the illness is organic, anger can play an important role in how we respond to it. If we get angry at having a physical sickness and being disabled, unable to work, with added financial burdens, the anger can prolong both illness and convalescence."[3]

What happens when this anger is not released? Your body remains prepared for action. Your heart is still beating rapidly, blood pressure is still up, and blood chemical changes are taking place.

JESUS AND ANGER

Jesus Christ experienced anger in His life, and for good reason. Norman V. Hope in *How to Be Good and Mad* gives some examples of Christ's anger.

"The gospel records make it perfectly plain that He could, on occasion, feel blazing anger and, feeling it, could and did give emphatic expression to it. For example, in Mark, chapter 3, the story is told of His healing a man with a withered hand on the Sabbath. When some protested that it was altogether improper to heal a man on the Sabbath, Jesus was indignant at their stubbornly perverted sense of values. The Scripture says that He 'looked round about on them with anger, being grieved for the hardness of their hearts.' In Matthew 23, the

---

3. Leo Madow, *Anger—How to Recognize and Cope With It* (Totowa, N. J.: Charles Scribner's Sons, 1972), p. 85.

account is given of Jesus' blasting the scribes and Pharisees, whom He describes as 'hypocrites' for the revolting contrast between their high religious profession and their low, irreligious practices. And in John 2 it is recorded that Jesus cleansed the Temple of its money changers, insisting that His Father's house must not be made a house of merchandise."[4]

Jesus experienced anger and felt free to let it show. He clearly and constructively expressed His anger.

CONSTRUCTIVE ANGER

It should be obvious from these examples that anger is not necessarily bad. The results of anger can be either positive or negative, constructive or damaging.

Anger is like gunpowder which, depending upon how it is directed, can blast away at injustices or can kill or maim the innocent.

When used constructively, anger can sometimes be an asset to a person. One who is angry enough may be able to accomplish great feats of strength which he would not otherwise be able to handle, such as raising a

---

4. Norman V. Hope, "How to Be Good and Mad," *Christianity Today* (July 19, 1968).

car off a loved one who is trapped underneath. Leo Madow in *Anger—How to Recognize and Cope With It* tells the story of a woman whose anger actually helped her function better.

"She had been called as a witness in a trial and was terrified at the prospect of being interrogated. Before she was called to the witness stand, she described her brain as being a 'sack of mush' and she was not sure she would be able to remember her own name. Meanwhile, the witness ahead of her in the case was saying things which were not true. As the woman listened to the testimony she became angrier and angrier. When she went on the stand, her mind was as sharp as a steel trap. She was able to testify very accurately, recalled many details that she was not aware she had known, and made a most effective witness. As she explained afterward, she became so angry at the lies of the previous witness that she forgot all her fears. It is worth noting that an extremely effective means of utilizing anger is in overcoming fear."

Madow explains further: "Constructively used, anger can give strength both physically and mentally. Such normal outlets for anger are dependent on several factors. First, the individual must not be overwhelmed by his anger, because he is then rendered ineffective. Second, there should not be so much fear of anger that it cannot be released directly, as it will then come out in unhealthy ways. Third, opportunities for some socially acceptable outlet must exist." [5]

Ephesians 4:26 tells us to "be angry and sin not." Earlier we saw that this is one of the passages where anger is legitimate. The word *angry* in this verse means an anger which is an abiding and settled habit of the mind, and which is aroused under certain conditions. You are aware of this kind of anger and it is under control. There is a legitimate reason for this anger. Your reasoning powers are involved and when reason is present, anger such as this is proper. The scriptures not only permit it but on some occasions *demand it!* Perhaps this sounds strange to some who have thought for years that anger is all wrong. But the Word of God does state that *we are to be angry!* as explained by Spiros Zodhiates in *The Pursuit of Happiness.*

"This, then, immediately disposes of the idea that the meek are passive persons who never get angry. There is no passivity in meekness. When the Lord Jesus Christ

---

5. As quoted in H. Norman Wright, *The Christian Use of Emotional Power* (Old Tappan, N. J.: Fleming H. Revell, 1974), pp. 111-12.

comes into our hearts. He does not go to sleep and put us to sleep. He becomes aggressively active within us.

". . . a Christian does and should get angry. But he must be careful to get angry at the right things and refrain from getting angry at the wrong things. Before he was saved and became blessed, his anger was sinful. Now, it must be righteous. Meekness is the sanctification of anger. It includes patience and long-suffering for personal affronts, with the willingness to speak out vigorously in defense of the Gospel. To get angry at what we should and when we should is a definitely Christian characteristic."[6]

As Dr. J. H. Jowett says, "A life incapable of anger is destitute of the needful energy for all reform. There is no blaze in it, there is no ministry of purification. If a city is to be purged from its filth it will have to be by souls that are burning with moral resentment. It is the man who is 'fervent in spirit' who will most assuredly 'serve the Lord.' 'The grass withereth . . . because the spirit of the Lord breatheth upon it.' The Church needs more of this withering breath and

6. Spiros Zodhiates, *The Pursuit of Happiness* (Grand Rapids: Wm. B. Eerdmans Publishing Co., 1966), pp. 263-64.

consuming energy that is born of holy wrath against all established wrong. We are taught in the New Testament that this power of indignation is begotten by the Holy Spirit. The Holy Spirit makes us capable of healthy heat, and it inspires the fire within us. The Holy Spirit never creates a character that is lukewarm, neutral, or indifferent."[7]

Paul actually commended the Corinthians in one place for their aroused indignation against the believer who had married his own mother (I Cor. 5:1-2, II Cor. 7:11).

This is righteous anger. It is not sinful when it is properly directed. Such anger must be an abiding, settled attitude of righteous indignation against sin, coupled with appropriate action.

There are three main characteristics of righteous anger. First of all it must be controlled. It is not a heated, unrestrained passion. Even if the cause is legitimate and is directed at an injustice, uncontrolled anger can cause an error in judgment and increase the difficulty. The mind must be in control of the emotions so that the ability to reason is not lost. "Be angry and sin not." Perhaps the way this is accomplished is related to the

7. As quoted in Zodhiates, pp. 270-71.

scriptural teaching in Proverbs: "Be slow to anger." This kind of anger is not a direct result of immediate frustration.

Second, there must be no hatred, malice, or resentment. Anger that harbors a counterattack only complicates the situation. Perhaps our best example of how to respond is Jesus' reaction to the injustices delivered against Him.

"When he was reviled and insulted, He did not revile or offer insult in return; (when) He was abused and suffered, He made no threats (of vengeance); but He trusted (Himself and everything) to Him Who judges fairly" (I Peter 2:23, Amplified).

"Beloved, never avenge yourselves, but leave the way open for (God's) wrath; for it is written, Vengeance is Mine, I will repay (requite), says the Lord" (Romans 12:19, Amplified).

The final characteristic of righteous anger is that its motivation is unselfish. When the motivation is selfish, usually pride and resentment are involved. Anger should be directed not at the wrong done to oneself but at the injustice done to others.

It is possible to confront another person without being angry. We need not confuse anger with confrontation and firmness. Anger usually springs from a desire to defend ourselves or to get someone to do what we want. You can share your feelings of frustration over the very same things, but in a nonviolent, nonattacking manner.

THE CHOICE IS YOURS

Once a person discovers he is angry, how can he deal with that anger? What choices are available to him? There are four basic ways to deal with anger.

One way is to *repress* it. Don't even admit that you are angry. Ignore its presence. "This repression is often unconscious, but it is *not healthy*! Repressing anger is like placing a wastebasket full of paper in a closet and setting fire to it. The fire will either burn itself out *or* it could set the entire house on fire and burn it down. The energy produced by anger cannot be destroyed. It must be converted or directed into another channel.

"One outlet for repressed anger is accidents. Perhaps you have met people who are *accident-prone*. Unfortunately, their accidents may involve other people as well as themselves. A man who is angry may slam a door on his own hand or someone else's. He may wash windows for his wife when he would rather be watching a game on TV and put his hand through the window. Perhaps his driving manifests his anger when he 'accidentally' runs over the rose bushes.

"Repressed anger can easily take its toll on your body by giving you a vicious headache. Your gastrointestinal system—that thirty-foot tube extending from the mouth to the rectum—reacts beautifully to repressed anger. You may experience difficulty in swallowing, nausea and vomiting, gastric ulcer, constipation, or diarrhea. The most common cause of ulcerative colitis is repressed anger. Repressed anger can affect the skin through pruritus, itching, and neurodermatitis. Respiratory disorders such as asthma are common effects and the role of anger in coronary thrombosis is fairly well accepted."[8]

In a newspaper report, "A Southland psychiatrist says that anger and unhappiness are responsible for most heart attacks."

Dr. Wallace C. Ellerbroek, a program director at Metropolitan State Hospital at Norwalk says, "learned control of such thoughts is much more important in prevention of heart disease than is strict adherence to a low-cholesterol diet."

8. Wright, pp. 121-22.

In an exclusive interview he also stated that "miserable people have a high cholesterol but happy people do not."

"If you check coronary victims," he contends, "you'll find they were either depressed or angry before their coronary."

"Cholesterol does play a role in heart disease," he explains, "but it is bad emotions, not diet, that send cholesterol levels soaring."

"For example, he likes to cite a study of Navy flight cadets. On the mornings the cadets were scheduled to fly, their cholesterol ranged from 400 to 650—extremely high. But on the mornings they didn't have to fly, their cholesterols were 140 to 165, he says—in other words, entirely normal.

"Any negative emotion—anger, depression, frustration, irritation, unhappiness, the blues—is going to affect the entire body and brain adversely to some degree, he maintains." [9]

Anger and hatred can lead to further complications. But so does repression. Repressed anger or anger held in or turned inward often turns into depression. In our unconscious attempt to handle the emotion, we bring harm to our own body.

9. Wallace C. Ellerbroek, "Anger—Sorrow Can Cost Your Life," (Long Beach, Calif.) *Independent Press-Telegram* (January 24, 1973), p. 60.

As David Augsburger writes in *Seventy Times Seven*, "Repressed anger hurts and keeps on hurting. If you always deal with it simply by holding it firmly in check or sweeping it under the rug, without any form of release or healing, it can produce rigidity and coldness in personality.

"Even worse, hostilities pushed down into the depths of consciousness have a way of fermenting into other problems. Depression, anxiety and eventually mental breakdown.

"Or repressed anger may come out indirectly in critical attitudes, scapegoating or irritableness. Often those we call 'good people' who harbor hostility will do indirectly and unconsciously what 'bad people' do directly and deliberately, because unreleased, buried anger colors their motive."[10]

Many large manufacturing companies dispose of their industrial waste material by pumping it into underground mines or abandoned wells. This works for a while but eventually it can pollute water systems or even burst out into the open through another channel. Our repressed anger is our own unrefined waste material.

Dr. William Menninger said, "Do not talk

10. David Augsburger, *Seventy Times Seven* (Chicago: Moody Press, 1970), p. 60.

when angry but after you have calmed down.
Sometimes we push each other away and the
problem between us festers and festers. Just
as in surgery, free and adequate drainage is
essential if healing is to take place." [11]

Anger is an emotion that must be
recognized and accepted. "When you repress
or suppress those things which you don't
want to live with," suggests John Powell in
Why Am I Afraid to Love? "you don't really
solve the problem because you don't bury the
problem dead—you bury it alive." God
created us with the capacity for emotional
reactions. We need to recognize and accept
our anger for what it is. Only then can we
learn to use it wisely and properly.

A similar way to handle anger is to
suppress it. A person choosing this means is
aware of his anger but chooses to hold it in
and not let people know he is angry. In some
situations this may be healthy and wise, but
eventually the anger needs to be recognized
and drained away in a healthy manner.
Otherwise the storage apparatus will begin
to overflow at the wrong time and place.

Often a person chooses to suppress his
anger when the person with whom he is
angry could react with more force or

11. William Menninger, "Behind Many Flaws of Society,"
    National Observer (August 31, 1964), p. 18.

authority. For example, an employer calls in one of his employees and angrily confronts him about some alleged problem. The employee feels his own anger rising but realizes that if he expresses his anger to his boss he could lose his job. So he suppresses his anger—until he arrives home. His wife greets him when he walks in the door and he replies with an angry snarl. This surprises her and she will either react by snapping back at him or by following her husband's previous example and suppressing her anger. But then her teen-age son walks in and she vents her pent-up anger upon the unsuspecting boy. He takes out his anger on the younger brother who in turn kicks the dog who bites the cat who scratches the three-year-old who takes out her frustration by pulling off the head of her Barbie doll! This simple process of directing your anger on a less threatening person is called displacement. It may help you for a moment but it can set up a long-lasting chain of events that infects the lives of others like an epidemic.

Guilt is another reason for displacing anger. If you are furious with your mother but believe that it is wrong to get angry with one's mother, you may find yourself exploding at other older women. Or you may use displacement to avoid humiliating yourself. You are traveling with your husband and trying to make mileage on a particular day. You take a wrong turn and go fifty miles in the wrong direction. You then project the blame onto your husband and accuse him of misguiding you.

Is the cause for your anger realistic? Is it reasonable? Is it born out of frustration? Does it come from unexpressed desires? Deal with the problem directly. If you have a disagreement with your employer over office procedures, the solution is not to go home and complain to your wife or to another employee. Talk with him and attempt to resolve the problem. If this is not practical, then you must put up with the situation and find other constructive outlets for your anger when it arises. The ideal solution is to practice various responses to your frustration.

If the cause for your anger is not legitimate, the problem is within you. If you get angry with your wife because she does not cook meals the way your mother did, then you had better recognize first of all that your wife is not your mother! Allow her to develop her own cooking skills and try some new recipes. Then learn to compromise on some of your expectations.

Dr. James Dobson was once asked the question, "Many psychologists seem to feel that all anger should be ventilated or verbalized. They say it is emotionally and physically harmful to repress or withhold any intense feeling. Can you harmonize this scientific understanding with the scriptural commandment that 'every man (should) be swift to hear, slow to speak, slow to wrath' (James 1:19, KJV)?" His response was very helpful: "In specific response to the question, we must harmonize the psychological finding that anger should be ventilated with the biblical commandment that we be 'slow to wrath.' Personally, I do not find these objectives to be in contradiction. God does not want us to repress our anger—sending it unresolved into the memory bank. Why else did the apostle Paul tell us to settle our irritations before sundown each day, effectively preventing an accumulation of seething hostility with the passage of time?

"But how can intense negative feelings be resolved or ventilated without blasting away at the offender—an act which is specifically prohibited by the scripture? Are there other ways of releasing pent-up emotions? Yes, including those that follow:

"By making the irritation a matter of prayer.

"By explaining our negative feelings to a mature and understanding 'third party' who can advise and lead.

"By going to an offender and showing a spirit of love and forgiveness.

"By understanding that God often permits the most frustrating and agitating events to occur, so as to teach us patience and help us grow.

"By realizing that no offense by another person could possibly equal our guilt before God, yet He has forgiven us; are we not obligated to show the same mercy to others?"[12]

It is interesting that some psychologists today advocate cutting loose with all of your anger regardless of the way you do it or the results. But other psychological research in the past few years indicates negative results of ventilating all of one's anger. The findings show that as the level of verbal aggression increases (anger poured out) the level of physical aggression increases dramatically. Discussing things calmly, getting information bearing on the issue, and calling for help from outsiders helps to settle the problems and keep the possibility for physical violence lower.[13]

12. James Dobson, *Dr. James Dobson Talks About Anger* (Glendale, Calif.: G/L Publications, Regal Books Division, 1975), pp. 16-17.
13. Murray Straus, "Leveling, Civility and Violence in the Family," *Journal of Marriage and Family* (February 1974), pp. 13, 21.

Suppressing anger does have some merit, however, especially if it helps you relax, cool down, and begin to act in a rational manner. The Word of God has something to say about this type of suppression.

"He who is slow to anger has great understanding, but he who is hasty of spirit exposes and exalts his folly" (Prov. 14:29, Amplified).

"A hot-tempered man stirs up strife, but he who is slow to anger appeases contention" (Prov. 15:18, Amplified).

"He who is slow to anger is better than the mighty, and he who rules his own spirit than he who takes a city" (Prov. 16:32, Amplified).

"Good sense makes a man restrain his anger, and it is his glory to overlook a transgression or an offense" (Prov. 19:11, Amplified).

"Make no friendships with a man given to anger, and with a wrathful man do not associate" (Prov. 22:24, Amplified).

"A (self-confident) fool utters all his anger, but a wise man keeps it back and stills it" (Prov. 29:11, Amplified).

"I (Nehemiah) was very angry when I heard their cry and these words. I thought it over, then rebuked the Nobles and officials" (Neh. 5:6-7a, Amplified).

"Understand (this), my beloved brethren. Let every man be quick to hear, (a ready listener,) slow to speak, slow to take offense and to get angry" (James 1:19, Amplified).

The individual who practices and exerts self-control will find that his anger level actually decreases. He will not become *as* angry as if he were to simply cut loose with his first reaction. A calm consideration of the cause for the anger and the results will help you handle the situation properly. Count to ten, taking a couple of deep breaths.

Expressing your anger is a third way to handle it. Some people think you should express exactly how you feel no matter what or who is involved. They feel this is psychologically healthy and necessary in order to live a balanced life.

There are many different ways to express anger. One is to react with violent passion, yelling harsh words, swearing, all with tremendous emotion. This can bring results but you may not care for them. If you are allowed the freedom to react in this way, shouldn't the other person have the same freedom to react to you in this manner?

But you can also express your anger by riding your bike around the block, digging in the garden for an hour, or beating on a stuffed pillow. You can write down exactly how you feel when you get angry, especially if it is difficult to verbalize your feelings.

These methods may sound strange but they should not be discounted. They have been used to help many people overcome their difficulties with anger.

If both you and your spouse are angry, it is better, if you are working it off physically, to do it separately. For some reason the anger disappears faster.

"The final method of dealing with anger is to *confess* it. This is . . . the best method, especially if it is coupled with an intelligent and healthy use of suppression or self-control. Confess the fact that you are angry—to yourself, to God, and to the person involved. Don't say, 'You're making me angry.' The individual is not making you angry. You are responsible for your own emotional reaction toward him. You could say, 'The way our discussion is going, I'm getting angry. I'm not sure that's the best reaction so perhaps we could start over in our discussion.' Or, 'I'm sorry but I'm angry. What can I do now so we can resolve our differences?' Try admitting and confessing your anger." [14]

What about talking things over while you are still angry? Doesn't this help? Actually it

14. Wright, p. 127

is very difficult to talk rationally about problems when you are angry. Exercise or relaxation is important before people attempt to resolve their differences. When people are calm, results are more evident. Confession and time may be the proper steps in the right direction.

Not all anger is sinful or wrong! Just the admission of being angry can help you release the feeling and get the message across in an acceptable manner to the person involved. David Augsburger writes about the problem in *Caring Enough to Confront*.

"Explosive anger is 'the curse of interpersonal relations.' Vented anger may ventilate feelings and provide instant, though temporary, release for tortured emotions, but it does little for relationships.

"Clearly expressed anger is something different. Clear statements of anger feelings and angry demands can slice through emotional barriers or communications tangles and establish contact."[15]

Don't you have to be angry in order to get your point across to others? They don't seem to respond unless anger is a part of the message! Believe it or not, it is possible to share a complaint or a criticism with another

15. David Augsburger, *Caring Enough to Confront* (Glendale, Calif.: G/L Publications, Regal Books Division, 1973), p. 49.

person in a calm, well-thought-out manner that will bring about more change than if you responded to him in anger. Many couples find healthy problem solving to be a major area of dissatisfaction in their marriages. Here are a few techniques which have worked for some. Perhaps these will help you avoid an angry explosion.

1. State the problem or complaint as soon as you can verbalize it. The longer you let the problem fester, the greater the possibility of resentment building and bitterness eroding the relationship.

2. Share your problem or concern in private so you don't embarrass the other person or cause him to feel that he must save face.

3. Let the person know that you are pleased with several aspects of the relationship before sharing what it is that bothers you.

4. Be sure to speak in the first person. Use "I statements" such as "I feel" and "I don't like to be" rather than "you are" and "you did this." "You statements" sound like accusations and quickly lead to self-defense and nonlistening, and perhaps even counter-complaining.

5. Pinpoint the actions that concern you and don't become a mind reader focusing

upon what you *think* the other person's motives are. Perhaps he was rude or didn't listen but do you really *know* that he had definitely planned to do that?

6. Comparing this person's actions and behavior with the failings of others does little to help solve the problems you are concerned about.

7. Forget the past. Talk about the present issue and make no reference to past difficulties.

8. Share only one complaint. It is too easy for the other person to feel dumped upon if he or she receives a barage of problems all at the same time.

9. Be sure to suggest in a non-angry, non-demanding, non-judgmental way some of the possible and realistic solutions that could be implemented.

10. Be sure you let the other person share his feelings and ideas about the problem that you are bringing to his attention. Even if he responds in anger to what you have said, his response is no reason for you to become angry.[16]

You can approach the other person by saying something like, "John, I have a

16. Adapted from John Lembo, *Help Yourself* (Niles, Ill.: Argus Communications, 1974), pp. 40-41.

problem. I'd like to talk with you about it as our relationship is important to me and this may help me. I feel . . . ." And after you share in this non-judgmental manner be sure to ask, "What do you think?"

The scripture says that a "soft answer turns away wrath." It also says that I am to "be slow to anger." I know it says that, but how can I do it? I have these people at work who every now and then get angry with me and start chewing me out with some complaint. I do get angry. How can I respond to them in a healthy way that would also be consistent with the teaching in the Bible?

Before some suggestions are given, remember, just because someone is upset with you, you don't have to become upset yourself, no matter how he says it or what he says.

1. If someone has a criticism to make of you, stop what you are doing and look directly at him. By giving your attention directly to him, the irritation may be lessened.

2. Listen to the person, let him talk. Proverbs 18:13 states: "He who answers a matter before he hears the facts, it is folly and shame to him" (Amplified). Try to hear what the person is really saying. Try to hear what is behind his remarks. You may just be

the object of all of his pent-up frustration, with nothing personal intended.

3. Accept the criticism as the other person's way of seeing things. From his perspective, his interpretation is correct. And he could be right, so don't write off the complaint. If he exaggerates, don't get hung up attempting to correct him at that time.

4. Don't accuse the person of being oversensitive or irrational. That won't help solve the problem that has been presented.

5. Don't bring up another subject or attempt to evade the present issue. Don't joke about the complaint because it could be very important to the other person.

6. Be open to the criticism and consider its validity before you respond. It could be right and this could be an opportunity for you to grow. You could even thank the person for bringing it to your attention, as this does help you know how the other person is feeling. Consider the following passages in Proverbs from the Living Bible before you make your response.

"If you refuse criticism you will end in poverty and disgrace; if you accept criticism you are on the road to fame" (13:18).

"Don't refuse to accept criticism; get all the help you can" (23:12).

"It is a badge of honor to accept valid criticism" (25:12).

"A man who refuses to admit his mistakes can never be successful. But if he confesses and forsakes them, he gets another chance" (28:13).

7. After the person has finished sharing his complaint with you, ask for an opportunity to respond to what he has said. First, restate what you heard the other person saying to you to show that you were listening and to make sure you understood everything. Then share what you feel and believe, and if the other person is correct, be sure to admit it. If you feel he is mistaken, you could defend yourself but how you share your feelings is very important. [17]

WHAT IS YOUR ANGER SAYING?

What is an answer for controlling and channeling your anger? What is your anger saying to you? What is its message? Could it be expressing a deeper hurt or desire? Behind angry looks could be fear and rejection. Underneath feelings of anger could be concealed expectations and subsequent

17. Adapted from Lembo, pp. 42-43.

frustrations. Inside angry statements could be hidden demands. David Augsburger suggests both a cause and a solution.

"You see, hostility has its root in reaction to love that is withheld or denied.

"The only cure, then, is in filling that void with love. God offers love. Unconditional love that will fill an open heart and heal the hurts.

"When you open your life to the love of God, you are unreservedly accepting God's love and God's loving way of living for yourself. Then the love of God goes to work penetrating the depths of your spirit with healing.

"A second step in opening your life to God is to absorb not only the assurance of His love and His loving spirit within you, but His Word. Read the Bible. Mull it over. Let it soak down deep into your mind. Memorize it. There is power in stocking your memory and your heart with what is lovely, good, wholesome, true (cf. Phil. 4:8).

"The truth of God absorbed into the mind and heart can act as a disinfectant to deal with the accumulated infections of our sinfulness.

"David, the ancient king of Israel, said, 'I store Thy word within my heart, to keep myself from sinning against Thee' (Ps. 119:11, Moffatt).

"Let the Word of God dwell in your heart and you will discover the strength it provides. You must experience it to understand it."[18]

For some people anger is sometimes a silent tiger pacing within them waiting for its victim. Ignoring and denying this tiger is not the answer. Neither is seeking to kill it.

Hear this parable.

"There was once a tiger keeper and a tiger cub who lived together. The keeper wanted the tiger for a pet, a friend. He fed him, walked him, cared for him. He always spoke softly, warmly to him. But as the tiger grew, his green eyes began to glow with hostility. His muscles rippled their warning of power. One night, when the keeper was off guard, a lovely girl happened by. The claws reached out. There was a scream. The keeper arrived too late. Then others felt the tiger's teeth—a boy, a man. And the keeper, in panic, prayed that the tiger might die, but still he lived. In fear, the keeper caged him in a deep, dark hole where no one could get near. Now the tiger roared night and day. The keeper could not work or sleep through the roars of his guilt. Then he prayed that God would tame the tiger. God answered, 'Let the tiger out of

18. Augsburger, *Seventy Times Seven*, p. 62.

the cave. I will give you strength to face him.' The keeper, willing to die, opened the door. The tiger came out. They stood. Stared. When the tiger saw no fear in the keeper's eyes, he lay down at his feet. Life with the tiger began. At night he would roar, but the keeper would look him straight in the eye, face him again and again. The tiger was never completely in his power, although as years passed they became friends. The keeper could touch him. But he never took his eyes off him, or off God who gave him the strength to tame the beast. Only then was he free from the roar of remorse, the growl of guilt, the raging of his own evil.

"Both keeper and tiger are you.

"God has not offered to kill your tiger. Death will do that all too soon. But His offer is and has been the strength to tame that evil within. To master it, before it masters you. He can and will set you free from its tyranny.

"Then He supplies the strength to live with your own passions, lusts, hostilities in check, so that the true you, made in God's own image, begins to live. And what a change. Christ called it a new birth. It's all that and more." [19]

19. Quoted in Augsburger, *Seventy Times Seven*, p. 63.

STEPS FOR HANDLING
FRUSTRATION OR ANGER

Here is a specific plan to follow in order to overcome frustration or anger. The following plan has worked for many.

1. Describe the behavior or attitude that you want to change (for example, anger, quarreling, yelling, etc.).

2. List several personal reasons for giving up this behavior or attitude.

3. Your own motivation to change is very important. From your reasons for giving up the behavior or attitude, select the most important reason. Write it down.

4. Begin to think about how you should change your behavior if you wish to succeed. Write these ideas down.

5. Adopt a positive attitude. What has been your attitude toward changing this in the past? Describe it. Indicate what attitude you are going to have now. How will you maintain this new attitude? Write down your answers to these questions.

6. Whenever you eliminate a behavior or attitude that you dislike, a vacuum or void will often remain. Frequently a person prefers the old behavior to this emptiness

so he reverts back to the previous pattern. In order for this not to happen, substitute a positive behavior in place of the negative. Describe what you can substitute for the behavior or attitude that you are giving up.

7. Read the scriptures again that are listed for this problem area. (A suggested listing is found at the end of this worksheet.) List the positive behavior or attitude that these scriptures suggest in place of the negative ones. Write out the way you see yourself putting this scripture into action in your life. Describe how you picture yourself actually doing what the scriptures suggest. Describe the consequences of thinking or behaving in this new way.

Here is a passage of Scripture to use for practice. (Many have found this passage very applicable to their lives and circumstances.)

EXAMPLE
Ephesians 4:31-32

Behavior or attitude to STOP	List the results of this behavior. Give several for each one.
Bitterness (Resentfulness, harshness)	

Anger (Fury-antagonism- outburst) **Wrath** (Indignation, violent anger, boiling up) **Clamor** (Brawling) **Slander** (Abusive speech)	
<u>Positive Behavior or Attitude to BEGIN</u> **Be Kind** (goodness of heart) **Tenderhearted** (compassionate) **Forgiveness** (an action)	What do you think would be the results of doing these three commands? List several for each.

Now write out the practical ways in which you see yourself doing the things suggested in the verse. Write down when and how you will begin and the consequences that you expect. Be very specific.

Now take the following scriptures that pertain to your area of concern and complete this procedure as outlined in Step 7.

Ephesians 4:26
Proverbs 15:1, 18; 16:32; 19:11; 29:11

DISCUSSION SUGGESTIONS

1. What do you feel most frustrated about?
2. What does God want you to do with your emotions?
3. Show others how you look when you're angry.
4. Describe how you feel when you are angry.
5. How do you handle guilt in your life?
6. What makes you feel really good about yourself?
7. What do you think God feels about you?
8. What are some things that we as Christians should be angry about?
9. What do you think is the best way to handle your anger?
10. Read Proverbs 15:1. Give examples of

this verse in action. How can a person be consistent in following the passage?

11. Read Proverbs 22:24, 25. What do you think this means for a family?

12. Describe how you can be "angry and sin not" (Eph. 4:26).

13. If you were honest and expressed your anger, how would the other members of your family react?

14. List as many causes for anger as you can.

15. The scripture says "Be slow to anger." Describe how this can be done.

16. Describe something funny that happened when someone was angry or upset.

DISCUSSION QUESTIONS AND ACTIVITIES FOR A GROUP OR CLASS SESSION

(Use some or all of these ideas, depending on the time available.)

1. Begin by asking everyone to write their own definitions of anger. (Provide paper and pencils.) Ask for several to give their definitions; do not share your definition yet. (3-5 minutes)

2. Provide every person with a blank piece of paper and with several crayons of various colors. Ask them to draw a symbolic picture of how they feel when

they become angry. When everyone has completed this, ask for some volunteers to show their drawings to the class, but do not have them explain the drawings. Ask for some opinions and observations from others as to the meaning of the drawings. Then have those who drew the pictures explain what they represent. (15 minutes)

3. Break into smaller groups of four or five to discuss these two statements. Ask each group to find scriptural teachings that answer each of the statements. (1) It is a sign of spiritual and emotional immaturity for a Christian to be angry with another person. (2) The Scripture teaches that we should avoid people given to anger. (7 minutes)

4. Describe the effect of anger upon the body. Use material presented earlier in this book. Read the story of Nabal in First Samuel 25 and expand upon that event. (5-10 minutes)

5. Ask the group to discuss Ephesians 4:26: "Be angry and sin not." Form small groups of three to discuss how a Christian can be angry and not sin. Ask each group to come up with specific examples. (10 minutes)

6. Discuss the New Testament words for

anger as described in this book. Read each verse. Then raise the question, "Doesn't the scripture seem to contradict itself? In one passage it tells us to be angry and sin not, and yet in another it says to put off anger and get rid of it." How do the three different Greek words used for anger in the New Testament help us answer this problem? (15 minutes)

7. Provide paper and pencil for everyone. Ask each person to write down the answers to these questions:

   (1) Describe the kind of anger that you usually experience, using the biblical descriptions of anger.

   (2) How do you express this anger?

   (3) What can a person do to make himself "slow to anger?" After they have had time to write their answers, ask for volunteers to share their answers with the entire group. Start with question 3, then ask for answers to questions 1 and 2. (20 minutes)

8. Share various methods of dealing with anger. (5-10 minutes)

9. Discuss the principles for dealing with anger as expressed in this book. (5-10 minutes)

10. Provide paper and pencils. Ask members to read Proverbs 15:1 and 29:11 and write out how they visualize themselves putting this passage into practice in their everyday life. After everyone has done this, break into small groups of three or four and ask everyone to share their answers. Then ask for some to share their responses with the entire group. Some may want to role play what they have determined to do. (30 minutes)

11. Close the session by reading Philippians 4:9, which emphasizes the concept of practice. Encourage the class to take the time this week to find other scriptures that deal with anger, and follow the same procedure of writing out and then visualizing the scripture as a part of their life. You can close by reading the quote of David Augsburger on page 48 and 49 of this book, followed with prayer. (5 minutes)

NOTES

NOTES

NOTES

NOTES